Baseball Legends

by Bob Italia

Published by Abdo & Daughters, 6535 Cecilia Circle, Bloomington, Minnesota 55439

Library bound edition distributed by Rockbottom Books, Pentagon Tower, P.O. Box 36036, Minneapolis, Minnesota 55435

Library of Congress Number: 90-083607   ISBN: 1-56239-008-2

Cover Photo by: Bettmann Archive
Inside Photos by: Bettmann Archive

Edited by Rosemary Wallner

Contents

Introduction

Baseball is a complex sport. To be a champion, a baseball player must possess strength, quickness, and agility—plus the determination to be the best. These five baseball players have shown their greatness, and dominated baseball during the years they played.

The batter, the catcher, the runner, and the umpire; all are part of America's favorite sport—baseball.

Hank Aaron played for the Atlanta Braves.

Hammerin' Hank

Henry (Hank) Aaron was born February 5, 1934, in Mobile, Alabama. His father worked in a shipyard as a boilermaker. Aaron had three sisters and had to share a bed with one of his three brothers. As a boy, Aaron was quiet and shy. But he loved baseball. Both his father and uncle played in the Negro League.

Aaron helped his family by chopping wood for the stove. The hours he spent handling the ax developed his muscles. Once his chores were finished, Aaron practiced his baseball skills by hitting bottle tops with a broomstick. Often he would practice well into the night by a streetlight.

In high school, Aaron played football and basketball. His high school had no baseball team, so Aaron played baseball in a sandlot league. He earned three dollars a game. Aaron was tall and strong. His quick wrists produced amazing bat speed that drove the baseball long distances.

In 1951, seventeen-year-old Aaron was asked to join the Indianapolis Clowns of the Negro American League. The team's manager offered him two hundred dollars a month. Aaron was excited, but his mother wanted him to finish high school. Deciding his mother was right, Aaron turned down the offer.

A year later, after graduation, Aaron joined the Indianapolis team as a second baseman. He was an instant success, as he led the league with a .467 batting average. The major league teams began to scout Aaron.

The next year during a doubleheader against the Kansas City Monarchs, Aaron got ten hits. The managers of the Milwaukee Braves were impressed. They bought Aaron's contract from Indianapolis and sent him to their minor league team. After a successful two years in the minors,

Aaron was called up to the Braves in 1954. The Braves put him in right field. He hit 13 home runs that season. His teammates called him the "Hammer" because of the way his bat pounded the baseball. Aaron told his teammates he wanted to be called Hank.

In 1956, Aaron had one of his best years. He led the National League in hitting with a .328 average and won the home run title with 34. Then in 1957, Aaron became a baseball hero when he won the pennant for the Braves by hitting an extra-inning home run against their rivals, the St. Louis Cardinals. While the fans went wild, Aaron was mobbed at home plate by his teammates. They carried him to the dugout on their shoulders. Aaron's heroics continued in the World Series. He had eleven hits and swatted three home runs as the Braves defeated the New York Yankees. Soon after, Aaron was named Most Valuable Player (MVP) of the National League. He was only twenty-three years old.

Aaron hit .326 the following year and helped the Braves capture their second straight pennant. Then in 1959, Aaron won the batting title again with a .355 average.

Aaron remained consistent throughout the 1960s. He averaged nearly 40 home runs per season while hitting around .300 or better. The home run totals began to pile up. In 1963, he had 300 career home runs. When the Braves moved from Milwaukee to Atlanta in 1966, Aaron had 400 home runs. He was certain to hit 500 homers, maybe even 600 by the time he retired. But no one thought he could break Babe Ruth's record of 714.

In 1970, Aaron collected his 3,000th hit. He switched from right field to first base so he would not have to run as much. Switching positions allowed him to play for many more years. By the time 1970 ended, thirty-six-year-old Aaron had 592 career home runs. Could he possibly catch the Babe's record after all?

In 1971, Aaron hit a remarkable 47 home runs—his best single-season total. The next year, he hit 34 homers. Suddenly, he was only 42 away from breaking Ruth's record.

Many thought Aaron was getting too old to keep up his consistent home run pace. But in 1973, at age thirty-nine, Aaron hit 40 home runs. One more and the Hammer would catch the Babe.

Hank Aaron collected his 3,000th hit
of his pro career in 1970.

Two more, and the record was Aaron's.

In 1974, Aaron wasted no time in tying the home run record. With his first swing of the season, Aaron hit a home run. Only a few days later, while the entire nation watched on television, Hank Aaron hit a line drive that cleared the left-field fence in Atlanta Stadium. Babe Ruth's home run record—a record everyone thought would remain forever— had been broken.

Aaron finished the 1974 season with 20 homers. He was then traded to the Milwaukee Brewers of the American League. In two seasons with the Brewers, Aaron hit 22 home runs. When he retired in 1976, Hank Aaron was first on the all-time list of games played, at bats, runs batted in—and home runs with 755.

Hank Aaron hits his 715th home run, breaking Babe Ruth's record.

The Kid

Ted Williams was born August 30, 1918, in San Diego, California. His father owned a tiny photography shop, but was always poor. His mother worked for the Salvation Army and was often away from home. Williams was usually on his own. He would often go to a nearby playground and play baseball.

The director of the playground noticed Williams's talent. He encouraged Williams to do push-ups to build up his skinny arms. Williams grew tall and strong, but remained skinny.

Ted Williams began his rookie season in the Boston Red Sox camp.

During his sophomore year in high school, Williams made the varsity baseball team. In three years as a pitcher and an outfielder, Williams had a .430 batting average. He already had the desire to become a professional baseball player. He also wanted to be the greatest hitter who ever lived.

A scout for the San Diego Padres of the Pacific Coast League noticed Williams. The scout signed him to a contract. Williams was only seventeen years old. In his first season with the Padres, Williams hit a respectable .271. But the following season, Williams started showing signs of greatness. That year, he hit .291 with 23 homers and 98 runs batted in (RBI's).

The New York Yankees offered Williams a contract when he was nineteen years old. It included a signing bonus of $500. Williams asked for $1,000, but the Yankees refused. Just when Williams thought he had blown his chance at professional baseball, the Boston Red Sox offered him a two-year contract worth $4,500—including a $1,000 bonus. Williams agreed.

In 1938, he reported to the Red Sox spring training. Noticing how young and thin Williams was, the equipment manager called Williams "The Kid." But the Kid did not do well in spring training. He was sent down to the team's Triple A club in Minneapolis, Minnesota. Eager to prove he belonged in the majors, Williams hit .366 with 43 home runs and 142 runs batted in. All three totals were tops in the minor league. Williams had won minor league baseball's Triple Crown.

Williams was in the Boston Red Sox lineup on Opening Day in 1939. He played right field. After striking out twice, Williams hit a double for his first major league hit. He finished the season batting .327 with 31 home runs. His 145 runs batted in led the league.

The following season, Williams hit .344 with 23 homers and 113 runs batted in. Though it was a good season, Williams was not satisfied. He vowed to do much better the next year.

Williams kept his promise. In 1941, he hit 37 home runs and drove in 120 runs. Better yet, Williams hit an incredible .406 for the year. Despite his remarkable accomplishments, Williams was not named Most Valuable Player.

In June 1941, Ted Williams led both the American and National leagues in hitting.

That honor went to Joe DiMaggio who had a 56-game hitting streak in 1941. The next year, Williams had another outstanding season. He hit .356 with 36 home runs and 137 runs batted in. He won his first major league Triple Crown.

Since America was involved in World War II, Williams enlisted in the marines after the 1942 season. He did not see any military action, but did not return to the Red Sox until 1946. That year, Williams picked up where he left off and hit .342 with 38 home runs. The Red Sox won the pennant, but lost in the World Series. Still, Williams was named Most Valuable Player for the American League.

In 1947, Williams had one of his finest years. He won the Triple Crown with a .343 average, 32 home runs, and 114 runs batted in. But again he lost to DiMaggio in the MVP balloting. Then in 1948, Williams won the batting title with a .369 average. He followed that up by capturing his second MVP award in 1949, hitting 43 home runs with 159 runs batted in.

In 1950, Williams suffered a major injury when he cracked his elbow in the All-Star Game. Still, he managed to hit 28 homers with 97 RBI's in just 89 games. Then in 1952, Williams returned to the Marines to fight in the Korean War.

In 1954, Williams was back in a Red Sox uniform where he maintained his .300+ batting average for the remainder of the 1950s. He won two more batting titles in 1957 and 1958. The title in 1958 was especially pleasing for Williams. At age thirty-nine, he became the oldest baseball player ever to win a batting crown.

After injuring his neck between seasons, Williams hit .254 in 1959. Now he was in his early forties, and thinking of retirement. But then, in 1962, he decided to give baseball one more try. In his last official at bat, Williams hit a home run. He finished the year with a .316 average with 29 home runs and 72 runs batted in.

After retiring, Williams spent his time fishing. In 1969, he came back to baseball to manage the Washington Senators. After three years of frustration, Williams got out of baseball for good and went back to his fishing.

In nineteen seasons with the Red Sox, Ted Williams hit 521 home runs and compiled an amazing .344 lifetime batting average. He won the batting title six times. Many believe that if he had not fought in two wars, Williams would have had more than 650 home runs and 3,000 hits. No doubt, Williams was one of the greatest hitters in baseball.

Joltin' Joe

Joe DiMaggio was born November 25, 1914, in San Francisco, California. His father, Giuseppe, was a fisherman. He owned a small boat and sold his daily catch on Fisherman's Wharf. He also had a four-room apartment and nine children.

DiMaggio could not help his father fish. He got seasick in the boat and did not like the smell of fish. Instead, DiMaggio sold newspapers and played baseball with his friends. Because he was from a poor family, DiMaggio did not have nice clothes to wear. When he got to high school and

Joltin' Joe DiMaggio

saw the other kids dressed in suits and ties, DiMaggio felt awkward and out of place. One day, he quit school and never went back. He began to sell newspapers full time. But DiMaggio was a quiet, shy boy and did not sell many papers. He got a job squeezing oranges at a soft drink stand. He quit after one day. Then DiMaggio became a delivery boy for a grocery store. After two weeks, he was back at the newsstand.

In 1931, DiMaggio signed up to play third base for a sandlot team in San Francisco. After eighteen games, DiMaggio had a .632 batting average. A scout for the San Francisco Seals of the Pacific Coast League spotted DiMaggio's talents and told him to tryout for the team. Since it was already late in the season, DiMaggio did not get to play until the final game. He played shortstop, hit a triple in his first at bat, then a double. Later, the Seals signed him to a contract worth $225 a month. Eighteen-year-old DiMaggio was stunned. He never thought he would ever make that much money.

DiMaggio was converted into a right fielder. He got at least one hit in sixty-one consecutive games—one of the all-time greatest baseball feats. During his hitting streak, DiMaggio packed the stadiums wherever he played. He finished with a .340 batting average and 28 home runs. He led the league with 169 runs batted in. The following year, DiMaggio hit .341. Afterwards, the New York Yankees bought DiMaggio's contract for $25,000 and invited him to spring training in 1936. Now DiMaggio would make $1,100 a month and would play left field.

DiMaggio got a hit in his first game as a Yankee. At one point, he had a sixteen-game hitting streak. But he was also a great left fielder. He often threw base runners out with his powerful arm. DiMaggio became a favorite with the fans. They called him "The Yankee Clipper" because he was so fast and graceful. Others called him "Joltin' Joe" because of his powerful hitting. As a rookie, he was named to the All-Star team. He led the Yankees to a pennant as they finished nineteen-and-a-half games ahead of the second place Tigers. DiMaggio hit .323 with 29 home runs and 125 runs batted in. In the World Series, DiMaggio hit .346 as the Yankees won. Then in 1937, DiMaggio was again an all-star, and the Yankees won their second straight World Series.

That year, DiMaggio batted .346 with 46 home runs. It was one of his greatest seasons.

In 1938, DiMaggio asked for a raise of an incredible $40,000. After much debate and criticism from the Yankees and fans, DiMaggio got his money. At the beginning of the season, the fans booed DiMaggio everywhere he went. They thought he was being paid too much money. But DiMaggio responded by hitting nearly .500. The booing started to fade. Eventually, the Yankees won their third straight World Series. For the season, DiMaggio hit .324 with 32 home runs.

In 1939, tragedy struck the Yankees. One of their stars, Lou Gehrig, was stricken with a fatal disease. Now DiMaggio had to carry the team. DiMaggio responded by hitting 30 home runs and a .381 average as he won the batting title. The Yankees won their fourth straight World Series—a record—and DiMaggio was named Most Valuable Player for 1939. The following year was an off year for the Yankees, but DiMaggio won his second straight batting title with a .352 average.

DiMaggio hitting a home run.

In 1941, DiMaggio accomplished one of the most amazing feats in baseball history. After suffering through a batting slump (hitting only .184 in twenty games), DiMaggio broke out of it on May 15 as he went 1 for 4. DiMaggio did not stop hitting until July 17. During that time, DiMaggio hit safely in 56 straight games. For the year, DiMaggio hit .357 and won the Most Valuable Player award for the second time.

But the United States had entered World War II in 1941. By 1943, DiMaggio had enlisted in the army. He did not return to the Yankees until 1946. DiMaggio got off to a great start, hitting 20 home runs in the first 41 games. But he was injured and finished the season with a .290 average—the first time he had finished below .300. The fans began to wonder if DiMaggio was on the decline.

In 1947, DiMaggio hit .315 and led the Yankees to another World Series title. Again, he was voted Most Valuable Player. In 1949, the Yankees won the World Series again, as Joe DiMaggio hit .346 for the season.

In 1950, DiMaggio signed a contract worth $100,000. But he was having problems with his throwing arm and his legs. People again began to wonder if he could still play. DiMaggio answered them by hitting .393 in the final months of the season, leading the Yankees to yet another World Series title. It was DiMaggio's ninth World Series. He had been on the winning team eight times.

During spring training in 1951, DiMaggio realized he could not perform as he once did. He finished the season with a .263 batting average—his worst—and only 12 home runs. The Yankees won the World Series, but eventually lost one of their greatest players, as DiMaggio announced his retirement that December.

During his long and outstanding career, DiMaggio had 2,214 hits, 361 home runs, and a .325 batting average. He played in ten World Series, winning nine of them. He was the star on the team that many consider the greatest ever.

The Say Hey Kid

William (Willie) Mays was born May 6, 1931, in Westfield, Alabama. Mays's mother was a former high school track star. His father worked in the toolroom of a nearby steel mill. He also was a baseball player in the Birmingham Industrial League.

When Mays was five years old, his father began to teach him how to play baseball. His father would take him outside and bounce a ball for his son to catch. They would practice for hours. He also took Mays to the ballparks with him where Mays would watch and learn about baseball.

Willie Mays played for the San Francisco Giants from 1950 to 1971.

When he was not chopping wood, cleaning the yard, or going to school, Mays played baseball with the neighborhood kids. When he could not find anyone to play with, Mays practiced by himself by throwing a ball against a wall and catching it. Mays could throw the ball harder than any kid on his block. Everyone was afraid to play catch with him.

After he turned twelve years old, Mays played with a semipro team in Fairfax, Alabama, called the Gray Sox. The manager put him in the lineup as a pitcher, but Mays's father did not allow that. He wanted his son to learn how to field and hit, so Mays was put in the outfield.

By the time he was fifteen years old, Mays was playing in the Industrial League with his father. The manager of the Birmingham Black Barons in the Negro League spotted Mays's talents and signed him up for $250 a month. The principal at Fairfield High School where Mays went to school did not like Mays playing professional baseball. But the Baron's manager made sure Mays went to all his classes. He did not allow Mays to play road games until the summer break.

Mays was a fabulous center fielder. He was fast and had a strong throwing arm. His hitting was good even though he had problems hitting a curve ball.

In 1950, a scout for the New York Giants baseball team became impressed with Mays. He signed Mays to a contract worth $250 a month. Mays also got a signing bonus of $4,000. He was sent down to the Giants minor league team in Trenton, New Jersey. Since Mays was only nineteen years old, his teammates called him "Junior." Whenever Mays wanted to get someone's attention, he would shout, "Say hey!" Junior was now called the Say Hey Kid. By the end of his first year, the Say Hey Kid hit .353— the best in the league.

The following year, Mays was promoted to Triple A ball. He pounded the ball for his Minneapolis team. Thirty-five games into the season, Mays had a .477 batting average. Then he got a call from the Giants. It was time to go to the major leagues.

After going 0 for 12, Mays hit a tremendous home run for his first major league hit. Then he went 0 for 13. He was sure he would be sent back to Minneapolis. The manager of the Giants, Leo Durocer, told Mays to relax. He told Mays to hit the ball to right field. The very next game, Mays went 2 for 4. Then he went 2 for 3 the game after that. The rookie slump was over. Mays was headed for greatness. The Giants tied the Brooklyn Dodgers for first place on the next-to-last day of the regular season, winning 37 of their last 44 games. The Giants won the pennant in a play-off. That year, Mays batted .274 and hit 20 home runs. He was named Rookie of the Year.

The following year, Mays was drafted into the army where he spent two years. When he returned in 1954, Mays picked up where he left off and led his team to first place by the middle of the season. Mays was named to the National League All-Star team, his first of twenty-four straight appearances. Mays finished the season with a .345 batting average and 41 home runs. Mays won the batting title that year, and the Giants won the pennant again. Then they went on to sweep the Cleveland Indians in the World Series. For his efforts during the season, Mays was named Most Valuable Player. In 1955, the Giants did not win the pennant, but Mays hit 51 home runs, tying a Giants record.

In 1961, Willie holds the bat that he used to score his 1,000th run.

In 1958, the Giants moved to San Francisco, California. Mays had another outstanding year, batting .347 with 29 homers. But the San Francisco Giants came in third at the end of the season. In 1962, a miracle happened. The Giants caught the Los Angeles Dodgers from four games back with only seven games remaining. Then the Giants won in a play-off, but lost to the Yankees in the World Series. Mays hit 49 home runs that season.

For the remainder of the 1960s, Mays continued his brilliant performance. In 1964, Mays hit 47 home runs. In 1965, Mays hit his 500th career home run, and finished the season with 52 homers while winning his second MVP award. By the end of the 1960s, Mays had 600 career home runs and over 3,000 career hits. But now, Mays was in his late thirties, and was slowing down. His batting average never went above .300, and his single-season home run totals never broke the 30 mark. Mays thought of retiring, but could not bring himself to quit the game that had been his life.

In 1971, Mays hit .271 with 18 home runs. The Giants started thinking of the future, and traded Mays the following year to the New York Mets. During the 1973 season, Mays decided to retire. And then suddenly, he found himself in one last pennant race. On September 25, the Mets held Willie Mays Night in his honor. Then the Mets won the pennant, putting Mays into his fourth World Series. In Game 2, Mays got the game-winning hit, a fitting end to an outstanding twenty-two-year career.

Willie Mays had a lifetime batting average of .302. He knocked in 1,903 runs and was the best defensive outfielder ever. His 660 home runs ranks third on the all-time list. If it had not been for the lost two years in the military, most people agree that Mays would have been the first to break Babe Ruth's home run record.

The Babe

George Herman Ruth, Jr., was born February 6, 1895, near the waterfront in Baltimore, Maryland. His mother and father were poor. They lived and worked in a saloon. Ruth was often left alone.

The waterfront was a tough place to grow up. Ruth skipped school often, and hung around with tough kids. They got into fights, drank alcohol, and stole things. "I had a rotten start," Ruth once said. "And it took me a long time to get my bearings."

In 1920, Babe Ruth began to play for the New York Yankees.

39

Because of his rotten start, Ruth became a juvenile delinquent. He was sent to St. Mary's Industrial School for Boys. His parents hoped the school would help him become a better person. St. Mary's was quite a change of life for Ruth. He had hours of religious and academic classes. Because he had difficulty adjusting, Ruth became one of the school's biggest troublemakers.

St. Mary's had a good baseball program. Brother Matthias taught Ruth how to play. Ruth learned quickly. Brother Matthias gave Ruth the love and attention he never got from his father. This helped Ruth turn his life around.

At St. Mary's, Ruth grew into a great athlete. At age nineteen, Ruth stood 6 feet 2 inches and weighed 170 pounds. He was the biggest boy at St. Mary's. He was also St. Mary's star baseball player.

Ruth was a catcher. But one day, Brother Matthias saw Ruth laughing at the poor performance of one of St. Mary's pitchers. Disappointed in Ruth's behavior, Brother Matthias decided to teach Ruth a lesson.

"You think you can do better?" Brother Matthias asked. "Then pitch."

"Me?" Ruth said. "But I don't know how!"

"Oh, but you must," Brother Matthias said. "Go out there and show us how it's done."

Having never once thrown a pitch, Ruth took off his catcher's gear and headed for the mound. "I didn't even know how to stand on the rubber," Ruth recalled. "Yet, as I took the position, I felt as if I had been born out there and this was kind of a home for me. It seemed the most natural thing in the world to start pitching—and to start striking out batters." Ruth became St. Mary's best pitcher.

Brother Gilbert, an athletic director at another Catholic School, wrote a letter to the Baltimore Orioles, a minor league club. He recommended that the managers take a look at Ruth. After receiving good reports from their scouts, the Orioles signed Ruth to a six-month contract worth $600.

Babe Ruth, the master slugger.

At the time, the Orioles were not a strong team. Jack Dunn, the team's owner, hoped that Ruth and his strong pitching arm would turn the Orioles around. In his first professional game, Ruth played shortstop, pitched two strong innings, and hit a long home run.

But like at St. Mary's, Ruth's outstanding performance on the baseball field did not follow him when the game was over. At hotels where the team stayed, Ruth often enjoyed riding the elevators. He would play with his friends instead of socializing with his teammates. But owner Jack Dunn did not care about Ruth's off-field behavior, as long as the young man played well. Ruth soon became known as Dunn's "Babe."

In his first start as pitcher, Ruth beat the world champion Philadelphia Athletics 6-2. Then he pitched a six-hit shutout over the Buffalo Bisons, winning 6-0. After the first few weeks of the season, Ruth was already recognized as a star. And the Baltimore Orioles were in first place. Still, the team was drawing small crowds and not making much money for Jack Dunn. To avoid financial ruin, Dunn was forced to sell some of his best players—one of whom was Ruth. Now Ruth was going to play major league baseball for the Boston Red Sox.

By now, Ruth was in his physical prime. He was still 6 feet 2 inches tall, but he weighed 198 pounds. In addition to having a blazing fastball, Ruth had developed a wicked curve. In 1915, his first full season with the Red Sox, Ruth's pitching record was 18-8 as the team won 101 games. The Red Sox then went on to defeat the Philadelphia Phillies and capture the World Series.

Throughout that championship season, Ruth was used primarily as a pitcher. But he was a great hitter as well, and he was often used as a pinch hitter. He hit four home runs for Boston that year and finished only three behind the league leader.

In 1916, Ruth became the best left-handed pitcher in the league, as he won 23 games and lost 12. The Red Sox won their second straight World Series. In 1917, Ruth's record was 24-13.

By 1918, the Boston Red Sox were trying to decide how to get Ruth's potent bat into the lineup. He was still a pitcher and did not bat in every game. Ruth's manager asked him to play the outfield when he was not pitching. Ruth hit eleven home runs in the final month and won the home run title.

Ruth probably would have become the greatest left-handed pitcher of all-time if he would have remained a pitcher. But in 1919, Ruth became a full-time left fielder. He hit an incredible twenty-nine home runs. Already he was becoming a legend.

But Harry Frazee, the owner of the Red Sox, was in financial trouble, and he wanted to trade Ruth. A mediocre team in New York, the Yankees, wanted to get better. They offered Frazee $100,000 for Ruth. Frazee agreed.

Ruth's fun-loving spirit blended perfectly with the Yankees. Ruth played right field for the 1920 Yankees. By mid-season he had 29 home runs and finished with a record 54 while batting .376. New York went wild for Babe Ruth. He was flooded with gifts and fan mail. New York Italians called him "the Bambino." Others called him "the Sultan of Swat." Ruth's accomplishments for New York gained him national attention, and

*1930—Babe bangs out a high one
against Philadelphia.*

helped baseball become America's favorite pastime.

In 1921, the Babe led the Yankees to their first American League pennant. He hit 59 home runs and had a .378 batting average. Then in 1923, Ruth helped the Yankees win their first World Series as he batted .393 and hit 41 home runs.

Ruth's success affected him in bad ways. He ate and drank too much, stayed up too late, and arrived at games too late. In 1925, Ruth missed two months of playing because of stomach problems. He was suspended for three weeks because of tardiness. Fans thought Ruth's career was over. Ruth vowed a comeback in 1926, and responded by hitting .376 with 47 homers.

Ruth's finest year was 1927. He hit 60 home runs and helped establish the 1927 Yankees as the greatest team ever. They won 110 games and finished nineteen games ahead of the second-place team. And they swept the Pirates in the World Series. The heart of their lineup became known as Murderer's Row. Lou Gehrig was one of the members. In 1928, Ruth hit 54 home runs with 142 runs batted in as the Yankees won the World Series again.

In 1932, Ruth played in his final World Series against the Chicago Cubs. During game 3 in Chicago, the Cubs and their fans taunted the Babe while he was batting. Angered, Ruth pointed to center field, then hit a home run to the spot he had pointed. His hit was one of the most memorable moments in baseball and became known as "the called shot."

Ruth's career began to taper off after 1932 as Lou Gehrig became the Yankee's best player. In 1935, Ruth signed with the Boston Braves and hit his final home run on May 25. That gave him 714 for his career—a mark that would stand until 1974.

Ruth retired after the 1935 season. He spent his time playing golf and making public appearances. Then in 1947, Ruth developed cancer. On April 27, the Yankees held Babe Ruth Day in his honor. Over 60,000 fans showed up to cheer their beloved Babe one last time.

On August 16, 1948, George Herman (Babe) Ruth died. But his legacy as baseball's greatest player lives on today.